Intermittent Sacraments

poems by

Mary Hills Kuck

Finishing Line Press
Georgetown, Kentucky

Intermittent Sacraments

Copyright © 2021 by Mary Hills Kuck
ISBN 978-1-64662-531-4 First Edition
All rights reserved under International and Pan-American Copyright Conventions. No part of this book may be reproduced in any manner whatsoever without written permission from the publisher, except in the case of brief quotations embodied in critical articles and reviews.

ACKNOWLEDGMENTS

The author wishes to acknowledge the editors of the following publications in which these poems appeared, some in slightly different versions:

Caduceus (2012), Advice from a Housewife
Connecticut Poetry Society Nutmeg Award Contest (2019), During that sleepless summer, Honorable Mention (published online)
Connecticut River Review, Bonding (1983), Deception (1984)
Main Street Rag, Bread (2020)
Simul: Lutheran Voices in Poetry, Grace (2007)
the Aurorean, Orphaned (2017-18)
Tipton Poetry Journal, The Luck of Pigs (2017), Woman on the Train (2018), At the Death of my Sister (2018), Glory (2018), Albino (2020).

Many thanks to Marianne McCartney, for her wise critique of this work, and to my poet friends in Jamaica, Connecticut, and Massachusetts.

Publisher: Leah Huete de Maines
Editor: Christen Kincaid
Cover Art: Sally Hills Strang
Author Photo: Greyson Photography: Deej Bhulasar
Cover Design: Elizabeth Maines McCleavy

Order online: www.finishinglinepress.com
also available on amazon.com

Author inquiries and mail orders:
Finishing Line Press
PO Box 1626
Georgetown, Kentucky 40324
USA

Table of Contents

Young Plum Tree 1

Grace 3

Advice from a Housewife 4

The Luck of Pigs 5

Bread 7

In the Sudden Felicity 9

In the Atrium at the Harvard Museums 10

Bonding 11

Deception 12

During that sleepless summer 13

Albino 14

A Poem 15

Fortieth Anniversary 16

Woman on the Train 17

At the Death of my Sister 18

Orphaned 19

Glory 20

For David, Sarah, and Benjamin

Sacrament: A visible sign of inward grace

Young Plum Tree

        I
The month of March collapses
into a single yawning day,
the hours drifting into each other
like dawn into dusk.

Who can remember when we first
learned the ailing world would seep
under our doors, into our bodies?

We stay at home, walk in woods,
neighbors nod, a beaver thrills,
a swan sails without a mate.

I dress in black beneath my stay-home clothes.

The numbers rise. Hundreds of thousands sick,
tens of thousands dead. *How long?*

        II
April. Time contracts, settles.
Hours tumble into routine.

I am making masks. In my left eye
you will see blood, and my smile
now can't conceal my tears.

Silent, masked, we glide
down the arrowed aisles,
spaces lie between us.

The numbers rise.
How long: weeks, or months?

III
The fickle season teases us with balmy sun,
then snows the greening garden, withers us with wind.
Yet just outside our window,
jonquils presage softer days,
chartreuse and rosy treetips promise leaves.
Our young plum tree sprouts hope
in delicate ivory blooms.

Grace

Three small pots perched on my sill,
a daughter's gifts to ease
long months of winter gloom.

Narcissus sprang right up,
extended emerald stalks,
fanned its waxy bride-white blooms,
scent not innocent nor sweet.

Amaryllis raised a thumb,
slowly issued chartreuse leaves
as counterpoise for swan-necked stamen's
bud that blushed and split and birthed
twin horns of scarlet passion.

The lily lingered.
I watched and watered,
impatient, dug the bulb.
Discovered roots, buried fast.
Blamed myself.

Today, two fragile tendrils
reach above pot's edge,
pledge reprieve.

Advice from a Housewife

Don't save the raspberries.
They won't freeze.
Next fall they'll thaw limp,
sour with the bitterness
of seeds held too long.

Eat them now,
succulent winebuds that burst,
spilling sweet liquor
in the curl of your tongue.
They're ripe, warm,
full of summer's first heat.
Savor their satisfying crunch.

The Luck of Pigs

I

I'm told the Chinese character for house
is a roof and underneath a pig.
The soothing snorts of future meals
and the warmth of a porcine body
help to make you feel at home.

Some Jamaicans keep a pig,
fatten it with scraps and let it roam,
to clean the gullies of their yummy trash.
A sow can breed a passel of pigs
for barbeque or gold.

My girlfriend's father tended hogs.
When eastern summer breeze
rustled doors and entered windows,
piggish scent pervaded every room.
"That," he said, "is the smell of gold."

My mottled gold glass piggy bank
held my saved-up cents; I should have
smashed it when it filled, but with a knife
I slid the coins out one by one
and saved that lucky pig.

In the Alps on New Year's Eve
we ate sow's ear with tangy sauce
that blasted through our noses, eyes.
Porcelain pigs in every shop
wished us happiness and luck.

II

A sow with brood in tow waddled
through a seminary gate, snuffled paths,
rummaged in the bins behind a class.
"She has a spirit," students whispered, pointing.
"See how pig and piglets follow her?"

In secret candled ring the girl lay prostrate,
arced by students' lamentations, hymns,
pleas and incantations to the demon,
"Let our comrade go!" But Satan knew the novices
weren't Jesus, hadn't yet his white-hot power.

Pig and piglets hovered at the edge,
resolved to do their duty and receive the spirits,
leap right off the cliff behind the sheds.
The demon snorted, did not budge.
In the morning shoats and students went to bed.

Bread

The widow was seeking sticks
for her last fire
for her last oil and flour
for her last bread
for herself and her son.
Then they would die.

Elijah asked her
to give *him* some
of that bread.
She did.
And did not die.

Her son lived. Elijah lived.
Every day the oil
and flour were there
for three and a half years
of drought.

This bread is not
the widow's recipe.
Flour and oil, yes.
But also water, sugar, yeast.
See how they cling together.

Under my fingers
the mass begins to grow.
I knead, pat, knead again,
slap it lightly, like
a baby's soft bottom.

Let it rise.
Punch it down.
Make the loaves.
Rise again, bake.
Incense swells, soars.

My offering.
Bless this bread.
Let me not die.

In the Sudden Felicity

In the sudden felicity of fall
leaves rustle with turning.

The maple says to the ash
Now is the time.
The ash says to the birch
Now is the time
and the birch says to the elm
Now is the time.

They plot to change their fertile green
into copper, coral, scarlet, gold.

Each year the blushing maple
at Spring Hill corner startles me.
I try to catch the simple pleasure,
wine-joy of those leaves, but
it seeps into winter, gone.

Give thanks for serendipity,
give thanks for delight.

In the Atrium at the Harvard Museums

Carlos Amorales, where's the wand
to ring these chimes?
Your graceful mobile
inches through the courtyard.
Dangling silver pendants
hang from measured limbs,
hooked and bent so triangles
can't touch, tease us
into wondering if
a strong breeze,
a deep breath,
might cause a pair to clash
and make a sound so joyful
that we'd stand and
climb on tables
and on shoulders,
using pens, umbrellas,
I-pads, or our phones,
bang upon these trinities
'til we could hear the angels
bing, ding, ring, sing.

Bonding

Silver is the cord that pulls me up to listen.
I trace the strand in bondage to your cry,
gather in the silver as I near you
curled in bed, afraid
of half-remembered dream.

In my lap I make a nest
and place you in it.
Mourning that my milk
no longer comforts,
I hold you to my empty breast,
wrap you round with silver threads,
rock you while the moon
spins lace upon us.

Deception

Winter has returned
after a two-week tease of spring,
and I know with relief that a few days more
I am sure in my vision of things.

Not that I don't love spring,
when it quickens and mellows the earth,
when it yellows a willow and whitens a bush
and brings to the world a new birth.

It's just that life is new,
and not being very astute
I might mistake a leaf for a flower
and expect it to bear fruit.

During that sleepless summer

we weren't the only ones
who feared our well had run dry.
Our neighbors' coughed up gritty silt
while our pump clanked and whined
at having to pull so deep.

We pinched off wilted blossoms,
clipped the daisies' ashy centers,
pulled the stalks of dying lilies,
watched the Rose of Sharon wither
with no drink to swell its blooms,
pricked our feet on scorched grass.

Thirsty deer in dark of night
skulked toward dewy flowers,
crushed my gift of giant ferns,
leaving brittle branches
spread like rusty bike spokes
on the crust of earth.

With daily pails of precious drops
we bathed the trimmed-off daisies,
worn-out lilies, trampled ferns.

Then, beneath the broken spokes,
mossy fronds poked through,
and the rain came to meet them.

Albino

In the balcony we sat, legs crossed,
urban-weary eyes lapping moonlight spilling
into wooded yard. Fireflies blinked in velvet air.
Crickets sawed, tree frogs bayed across the spread.

Some low leaves shivered, and a ghostly figure
moved along the line of trees. We followed it,
eyes wide, to the edge of swamp. *Perhaps*, you said,
a big white cat, but likely not a crouching man.

It rustled into brush and we leaned together,
marvelling that we could share
this woodland with the wildlife and the grass.
The moon arced; darkness wrapped us.

Later in the week I got up early, stepping lightly
to the rim of the ravine, rising sun behind me
rouging trees and sky. I wanted to give thanks
for all the green, the swampy pond, the wild.

As I breathed the life of woods, I sensed
a being at my side and looked down into grass.
A pearly face with pudgy cheeks and feather tail
locked me with her pink-tinged eyes.

Her body white, her whiskers milky mild, the beast
bewitched me with her grace. At last I saw the danger
that the alabaster skunk-like shape conferred.
We both stood absolutely still, silently evaluating risk.

I waited for the dreaded turn of tail, but, what a gift,
she trusted me and slipped back down the cliff.

A Poem

All my little joys or sorrows needn't be immortal.
I just want to love the wilful seasons, mourn my losses,
without seeking proper words to etch them on the glass
through which I see the world.

But, look, the super moon here beams so bright
it brings me out of sleep to lift the window blind
and see the rocks and sprouting flowers doused in light.
Tufts of clouds the wind has pulled apart have blown
across the indigo to shroud the dazzling brilliance
of that radiant moon. To no avail—it shines right through,
causing leafless branches to trace their fragile patterns
on the dusty pale blue puffs.

I wonder if this silver washing over me
and on my chair is at last a longed-for blessing
that I cannot comprehend. I'll sit and let it gleam,
hoping delicate slivers will linger in the morning
to remind me of the joy of this brief poem.

Fortieth Anniversary

Lay your head upon my breast,
my dear, and listen to the way
my heart is talking in the
measured sighs and gurgles
of the past and present pleasures
of the life we share together,
the rhythms and the rests,
the as-yet steady pauses
in our pulsing daily traffic
that unless we are together
we simply cannot hear.

Woman on the Train

No one on this train knows about my heart.
If any one of them should look up
from their phones, or papers,
tired re-runs of their workday,
they would see me crushed
between two passengers.

They would not know my heart
is racing, beating syncopated rhythms
like exotic conga drums,
suggesting wild, enticing dance.

They would not know
that I have tried but failed
to settle down this heart,
and now with my life
moving all the margins in,
I think I might just yield and
start to boogie to its beat.

What would they think
if I stood up here in this aisle
and moved my ageing torso
to the music only I can hear?
If I jived, arms raised, up and down the car
to the door and back?

Maybe I'll just caper to the exit,
cha-cha to the escalator,
whirl up onto Park Street,
twist right out of sight.

At the Death of My Sister

Lord, you didn't shine me up
the way you polished Moses.
He too thought he was unfit
and didn't even seek you
like I do.

You sought *him* out.
You lighted up that bush for him,
coiled his serpent staff,
withered white, then healed his hand.
He had to know that it was you.

Forty days you spent with him,
burnished him with all those words
while he produced that famous stone,
and then he shone,
with your pure light.

At the brink of her great glory,
 (who would find it if not she),
in that final wisp of air,
could you not have kindled her
and singed me too?

Orphaned

In Funks Grove
thick flakes
fill empty spaces
where last week

sunlight streamed
through amber leaves
to the stone

till now
engraved
on only one side.

Glory

If I go first, I'll take my phone,
you know, the pink one
with the little floral strap?

When you reach the glitzy gate
just text to say you're here
and I'll whirl out to meet you.

You'll know me—I'll be in white
like all the rest, but only I
will have that phone.

Take the strap,
I'll pull you through
sing glory, glory, glory.

Mary Hills Kuck was born in Missouri and spent her early years in small Midwestern towns, where her father served as a Presbyterian minister. After living for a year in Germany, she taught English and German in St. Louis and in various schools and institutions on the East Coast. For 23 years she taught at the United Theological College of the West Indies and the Vocational Training and Development Institute in Kingston, Jamaica. Living now with family in Massachusetts, she still relishes the friendships and insights she gained during the years in Jamaica.

She has published in numerous journals, most recently in *Slant, Burningword Literary Journal, Connecticut River Review,* and *Tipton Poetry Journal.* One of her poems has been nominated for the Pushcart Prize. She sees her writing as having a voice in the world that reflects the sacredness of our connection to nature and to each other, as well as the need for social justice, empathy, and change.

www.ingramcontent.com/pod-product-compliance
Lightning Source LLC
LaVergne TN
LVHW041523070426
835507LV00012B/1790